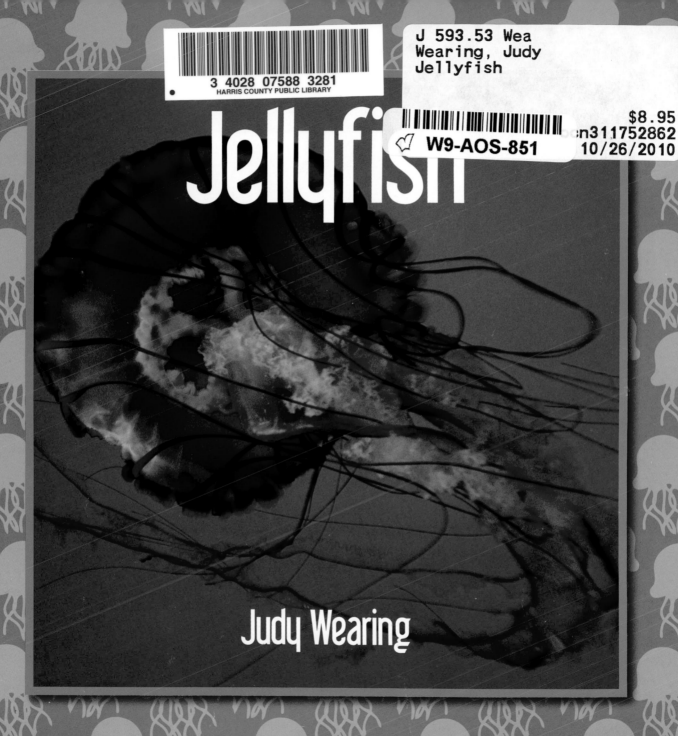

Jellyfish

Judy Wearing

Published by Weigl Publishers Inc.
350 5th Avenue, Suite 3304, PMB 6G
New York, NY 10118-0069
Website: www.weigl.com

Library of Congress Cataloging-in-Publication Data available upon request.
Fax 1-866-44-WEIGL for the attention of the Publishing Records department.

ISBN 978-1-60596-100-2 (hard cover)
ISBN 978-1-60596-101-9 (soft cover)

Printed in China
1 2 3 4 5 6 7 8 9 0 13 12 11 10 09

Editor: Heather C. Hudak
Design and Layout: Terry Paulhus

All of the Internet URLs given in the book were valid at the time of publication. However, due to the dynamic nature of
the Internet, some addresses may have changed, or sites may have ceased to exist since publication. While the author
and publisher regret any inconvenience this may cause readers, no responsibility for any such changes can be accepted
by either the author or the publisher.

Every reasonable effort has been made to trace ownership and to obtain permission to reprint copyright material. The
publishers would be pleased to have any errors or omissions brought to their attention so that they may be corrected
in subsequent printings.

Weigl acknowledges Getty Images as its primary image supplier for this title.

CONTENTS

What is a Jellyfish?

Have you ever jiggled a bowl of jello? Jellyfish are jiggly like jello. This is because they have jelly inside their bodies.

Jellyfish are a kind of **ocean** animal, but they are not fish. They have soft bodies and long **tentacles**.

There may be more than 2,000 kinds of jellyfish. About 200 are known to humans.

5

Around the World

Did you know that oceans cover about 75 percent of Earth? Jellyfish make their homes in oceans all over the world. They live in cold **arctic** waters and warm **tropical** waters.

Jellyfish can be found near the shore and in the darkest, deepest parts of the ocean. There is even a type of jellyfish that lives in lakes and ponds.

Open Umbrellas

How do you stay dry when it rains? Do you use an umbrella? Many jellyfish are shaped like an open umbrella.

The part of a jellyfish that looks like the top of an umbrella is called the bell. The mouth and stomach of the jellyfish are found inside the bell. The bell is covered in a thin skin that is filled with a type of jelly.

Jellyfish do not have a heart, brain, or bones.

9

Catch of the Day

What are the long, stringy parts that hang from the bell of the jellyfish? These are tentacles. They are used to catch food.

Jellyfish eat small animals that touch their tentacles. The tentacles shoot out tiny, poison **darts** almost as fast as a bullet. The darts work like a doctor's needle to poison the animal. Then, the jellyfish eats it.

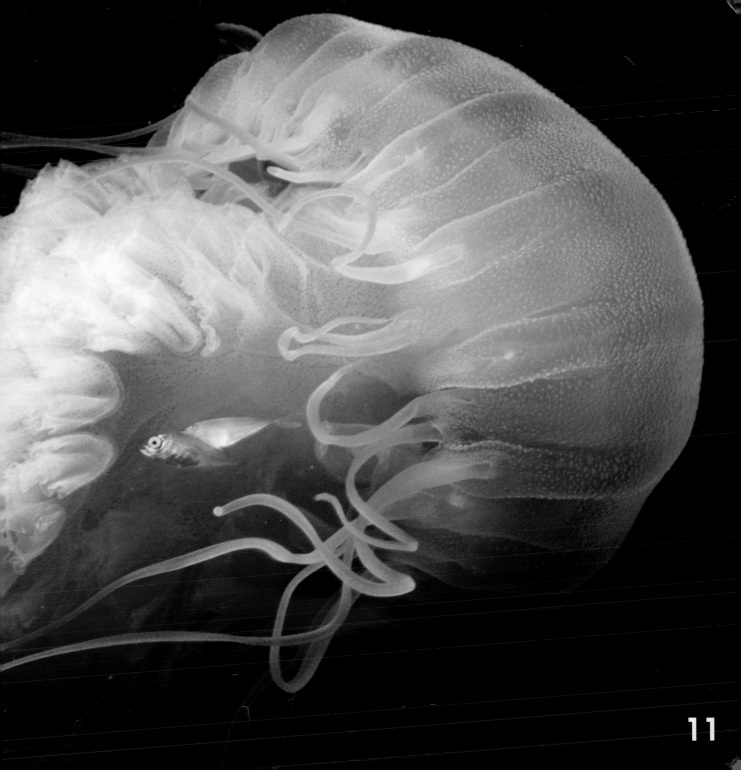

11

Moving Right Along

How many people live in your house? Did you know that one million jellyfish can live together. They often **float** in a big **swarm**.

Jellyfish float easily. They can travel a long way by floating in the moving ocean. Jellyfish also can push themselves through the water.

To do this, jellyfish squeeze a ring of muscles on their bell. This pushes water out of the bell and moves them forward.

Baby Blobs

Do you look like your mom or dad? Young jellyfish do not look like their parents. They look like small bowling pins and are called polyps. Polyps attach to rocks at the bottom of the sea. Some stay there for many years.

One polyp can become many jellyfish. Over time, a polyp will look like a stack of **frisbees**. Each disk is a tiny jellyfish. One by one, the jellyfish leave the polyp and float away. Adult jellyfish live only a few months.

Big or Small

Did you know that the smallest jellyfish are the size of a coin? They are about 0.5 inch (12 millimeters) in size.

The largest jellyfish is called the lion's mane. It grows up to 8 feet (2.4 meters) wide. Its tentacles can be as long as 100 feet (30.5 m).

Watch Out!

What happens if you touch a jellyfish? If you touch a jellyfish's tentacle, it will **sting** you. Even a dead jellyfish can sting.

Most jellyfish stings only harm small fish and animals. Still, a few jellyfish have stings that can hurt people. If you see a jellyfish, it is best to stay away.

Some jellyfish are famous for their sting. The sea wasp is a jellyfish that lives in Australia. Its sting can kill a person in minutes.

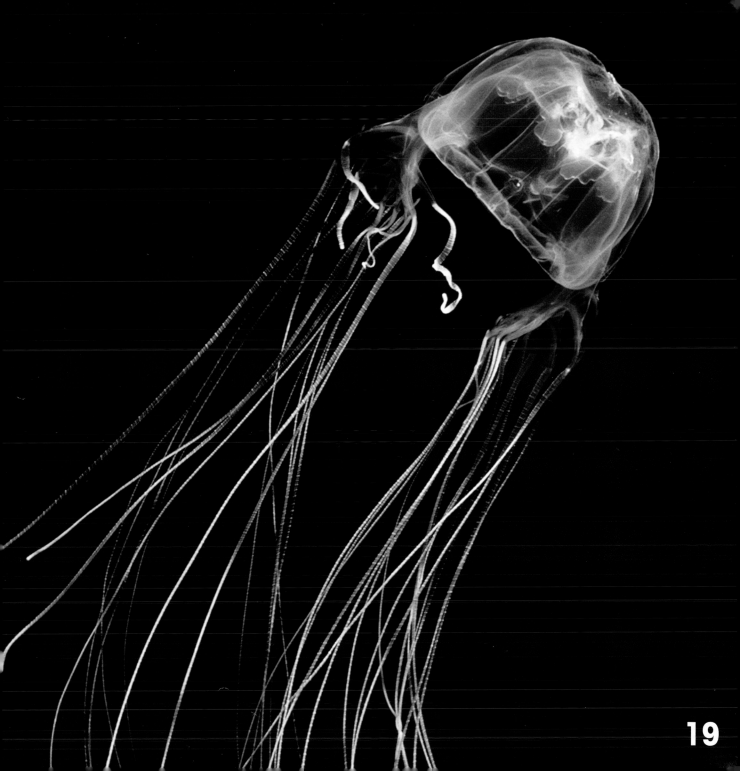

19

All in a Look

Did you know that jellyfish are made mostly of water? This makes their bodies look clear. It is easy for them to hide from other animals.

Some jellyfish have a bit of color. They can be pink, purple, yellow, red, green, or many other colors. Their bright colors warn other water animals to stay away.

Move Like a Jellyfish

Supplies
an umbrella, long lengths of streamers, tape, balloons, an open area

1. Tape the streamers around the edge of the open umbrella so that it looks like a jellyfish with tentacles.

2. Count to three, and close your umbrella like a jellyfish closing its bell. What do you feel?

3. Blow up the balloon. Do not tie it closed. Instead, keep the air from escaping by holding it closed with your hand.

4. Let go of the balloon. What happens?

5. A jellyfish moves just like the balloon. When it closes its bell, it pushes water out, just like air is pushed out of the umbrella and the balloon. The air pushes the balloon forward, just like the water pushes the jellyfish forward.

6. Being careful of others around you, open and close your umbrella and pretend you are a jellyfish swimming through the ocean.

Find Out More

To learn more about jellyfish, visit these websites.

National Geographic Kids
www.nationalgeographic.
com/ngkids/9608/jellyfish

Jewels of the Sea
www.aquarium.org/
jellies/index.htm

Fort Wayne Children's Zoo
www.kidszoo.org/animals/
moonjellyfish.htm

**U.S. Department of
Natural Resources**
www.dnr.sc.gov/marine/pub/
seascience/jellyfi.html

Sea Science

An Information/Education Series from the Marine Resources Division

Jellyfish

Few marine creatures are as mysterious and intimidating as jellyfish. Though easily recognized, these animals are often misunderstood. Some bathers and beachcombers react with fear upon encountering these invertebrates, but, in fact, most jellyfish in South Carolina waters are harmless. This article was prepared to help coastal residents and vacationers learn the difference between the jellyfish to avoid and the ones you can safely ignore.

Jellyfish are members of the phylum Cnidaria, a structurally simple marine group of both fixed and mobile animals: sea anemones, sea whips, corals and hydroids are polyps that grow attached to rocks or other hard surfaces; jellyfish and colonial siphonophores like the Portuguese man-of-war are mobile (either actively swimming or subject to winds and currents). Inherent to both types of life history is their radial symmetry (body parts radiating from a central axis). This symmetry allows jellyfish to detect and respond to food or danger from any direction.

Instead of a brain, jellyfish possess an elementary nervous system, or nerve net, which consists of receptors capable of detecting light, odor and other stimuli and coordinating appropriate responses.

Jellyfish are composed of an outer layer (epidermis), which covers the external body surface, and an inner layer (gastrodermis), which lines the gut. Between the epidermis and gastrodermis is a layer of thick elastic jellylike substance called mesoglea ("middle jelly"). Jellyfish have a simple digestive cavity, (coelenteron), which acts as a gullet, stomach and intestine, with one opening for both the mouth and anus. Four to eight oral arms are located near the mouth and are used to transport food that has been captured by the tentacles to the mouth.

Jellyfish come in a wide variety of sizes, shapes and colors. Most are semi-transparent or glassy and bell-shaped, measuring less than an inch to more than a foot across the bell, although some may reach seven feet in diameter. The tentacles of some jellyfish can reach lengths greater than 100 feet. Regardless of their size or shape, most jellyfish are very fragile, often containing less than 5% solid organic matter.

Jellyfish inhabit every major oceanic area of the world and are capable of withstanding a wide range of temperatures and salinities. Most live in shallow coastal waters, but a few inhabit depths of 12,000 feet!

Jellyfish Information
Food
Life Cycles
Local Jellyfish
Locomotion
Prevention
Treatment of Sting
Saltwater Fishing
Conservation & Ethics
Venom Apparatus

Video of Ctenophor comb jelly

General Medusa Body Plan

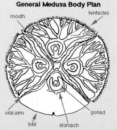

Glossary

arctic: the area around the North Pole, where it is very cold

darts: small, pointed items that are thrown

float: to rest in place in water without sinking

frisbees: plastic disks

ocean: the very large areas of salt water on the surface of Earth

sting: a sharp, pointed part of an animal that pierces the skin and causes sharp pain

swarm: a large group

tentacles: long, slim, flexible parts of an animal

tropical: the area around the equator where it is very warm

Index